John Himmelman

MOUSE in a MEADOW

Charlesbridge

For Chloe, my sweet little niece
—J. H.

Special thanks to Dr. David R. Foster,
director of the Harvard Forest,
Petersham, Massachusetts.

Published by Charlesbridge
85 Main Street
Watertown, MA 02472
(617) 926-0329
www.charlesbridge.com

Library of Congress Cataloging-in-Publication Data
Himmelman, John
    Mouse in a meadow / John Himmelman
        p. cm.
    ISBN 1-57091-520-2 (reinforced for library use)
    ISBN 1-57091-521-0 (softcover)
1. Meadow animals—Juvenile literature. 2. Meadow ecology—
Juvenile literature. I. Title.
QL115.5.H56 2005
578.74'6—dc22   2004003306

Printed in Korea
(hc) 10 9 8 7 6 5 4 3 2 1
(sc) 10 9 8 7 6 5 4 3 2 1

Illustrations done in watercolor on Arches 140 watercolor paper
Display type and text type set in Caxton and Barcelona
Color separated, printed, and bound by Sung In Printing, South Korea
Production supervision by Brian G. Walker
Designed by Diane M. Earley

A mouse is in a meadow.

The mouse nibbles on nutsedge nutlets.

A leafhopper resting in the nutsedge jumps to a patch of grass.

A snake is hunting there.

The snake startles a moth, who flies away.

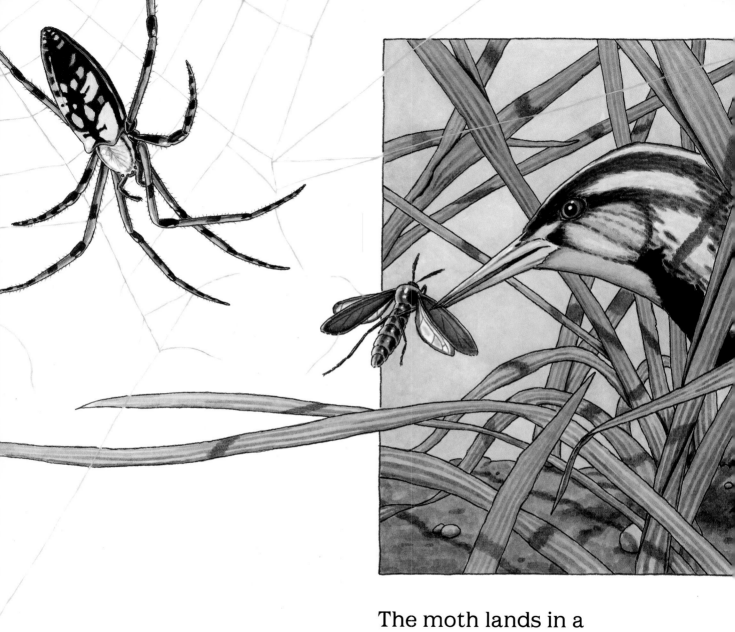

The moth lands in a
spider's web.

A meadowlark beats her to it. No meal for the spider.

The spider repairs her web.

An ambush bug waits in a yarrow flower.

A butterfly lands on the flower and is caught.

A young artist draws the scene.

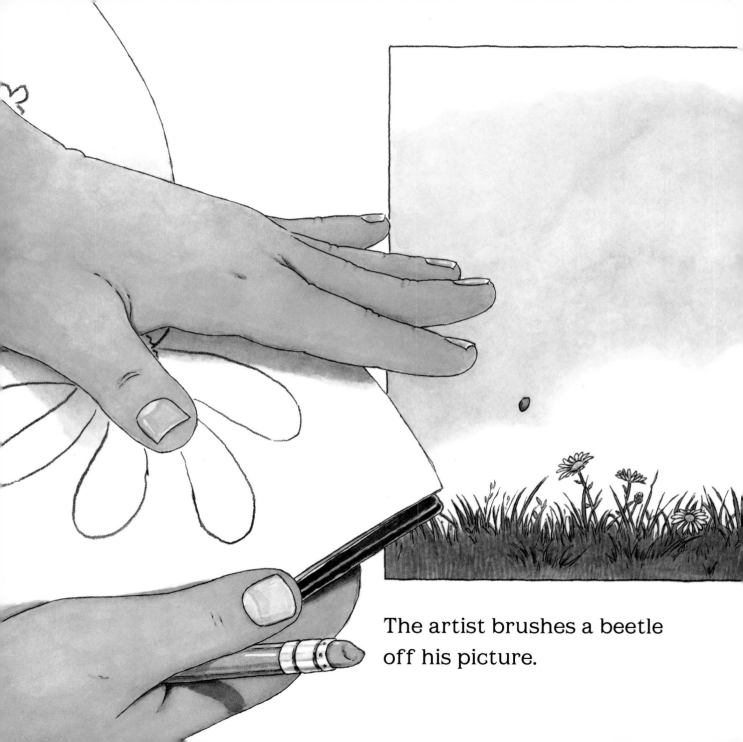

The artist brushes a beetle
off his picture.

The beetle flies to a milkweed plant.

A frog hops under the plant. Coneheads jump out of its way.

One conehead lands in a spittlebug's bubbles.

The spittlebug makes more
bubbles to hide again.

A bobolink watches. Either insect would taste good.

The bobolink hears
a rustle.

A weasel is looking for something to eat.

It knows there is a mouse
hiding in the meadow.

Can you find this spider and these insects?

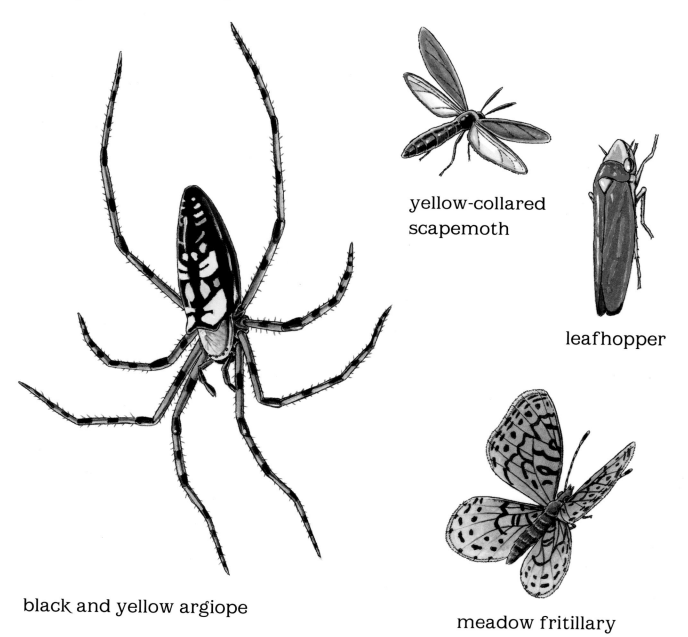

yellow-collared
scapemoth

leafhopper

black and yellow argiope

meadow fritillary

meadowhawk (dragonfly)

spittlebug

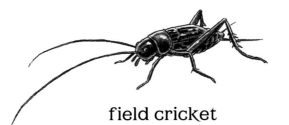

field cricket

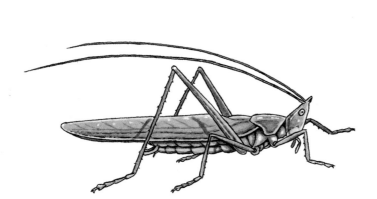

eastern swordbearer (conehead)

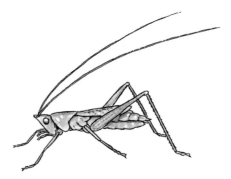

meadow katydid

Here are a few more insects to find.

milkweed beetle

ambush bug

robberfly

Can you find this amphibian?

leopard frog

And this reptile?

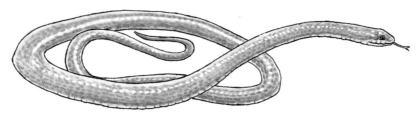

green snake

Here are three mammals to look for.

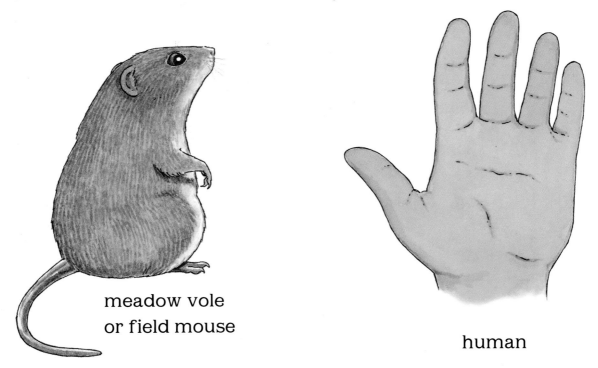

meadow vole
or field mouse

human

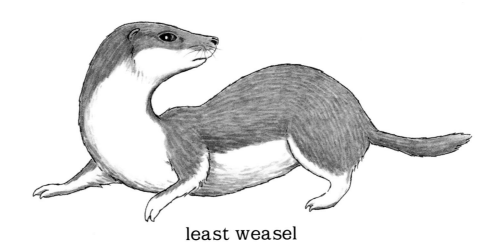

least weasel

Can you find these birds?

meadowlark

bobolink

field sparrow

red-tailed hawk

Can you find these plants?

Virginia meadowbeauty

oxeye daisy

purple coneflower

black-eyed susan

Here are a few more plants to find.

red clover

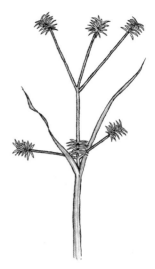

yellow nutsedge

bush clover

rye grass

dwarf cinquefoil

meadowsweet

yarrow

common milkweed

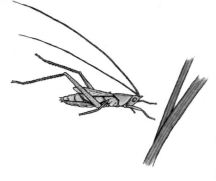

What is a meadow? Meadows are habitats made up mostly of grass, grass-like plants, and wildflowers. They can be wet or dry, near saltwater, in the mountains, or even in your own backyard. Within a meadow are many smaller habitats—leaves, rocks, and tunnels—which are home to a variety of creatures. Native grasses tend to grow in clumps. This leaves openings for other plants and flowers to sprout from. In the eastern United States, most meadows are created by humans. Any open grassy area we create will revert back to forest if left alone long enough. Keeping a meadow open requires either mowing it every year or two or, as the Native Americans practiced, burning it.

You can create your own meadow by planting native grasses and wildflowers. Let it grow wild and mow it only once a year in the early spring. Animals have a way of finding these habitats, and your meadow will soon be filled with wonderful creatures to draw and study.

Resources

For younger readers

Hunter, Anne. *What's in the Meadow?* Boston: Houghton Mifflin, 2000.

Nadeau, Isaac. *Food Chains in a Meadow Habitat.* New York: Powerkids Press, 2002.

Paul, Tessa. *In Fields & Meadows.* New York: Crabtree Publishing, 1997.

For older readers

Martin, Patricia A. Fink. *Prairies, Fields, and Meadows* (Exploring Ecosystems). New York: Franklin Watts, 2002.

Schwartz, David M. *The Hidden Life of the Meadow,* photographs by Dwight Kuhn. New York: Crown, 1988.

On the Internet

Teachers can visit The Wildlife Habitat Council's site at **http://www.wildlifehc.org/managementtools/backyard-pollinators.cfm** for lesson plans on exploring meadows.

Visit **www.eNature.com** for information on meadows and many of the species in this book.

Check out "Creating Wildflower Meadows for Wildlife" at **http://www.deq.state.la.us/assistance/earthday/meadows.htm.** The site focuses on Louisiana, but the information applies to much of the United States.